WHERE'S MY
Birth Father?

DEBORAH RIGGS

Fulton Books, Inc.
Meadville, PA

Published by Fulton Books 2021

ISBN 978-1-63710-456-9 (paperback)
ISBN 978-1-63710-457-6 (digital)

Printed in the United States of America

CHAPTER 1

Many, many years ago, on a hot summer day in June of 1960, I was born to a young, happy couple named William (Bill) Eugene and LaVern Ruth Bryant Dobbs. I also have a big brother; his name is Larry Eugene, but for some unknown reason, everyone calls him Butchie. He is a year and a half older than I am. I would say that my parents were very happy to have a son first so he could watch over me and be my hero when we started school.

Needless to say, I don't remember any of this because I was just a little baby, but I have so many pictures of my family and friends; it looks as if we had a wonderful, happy life. Looking through all the pictures with my brother, there were so many people who we didn't know and wonder if they were family or friends. It seems as if we had so many memories. We would love to get together with anyone who remembers our family and exchange stories. I believe that would be a great start in getting to know family or friends.

According to my birth certificate, we lived at 2959 Colerain Avenue, Cincinnati, Ohio, when I was born, but of course, I don't remember that. I now live at 255 Mehaffey Road, Powell, Tennessee 37849, and my phone number is 865-361-1832.

In all the pictures I have been looking through, we seem to be just like any other family. We had a very nice house which was beautifully decorated, had many family pictures on the walls, lots of toys, and a large yard to play in. It looks like we had everything we could ever want or need. One thing I can say is that our pictures indicate that we were a very fun, loving, and caring family.

CHAPTER 2

My Family

I had the most beautiful mother in the world. She was a very small, petite, young lady. She always looked as if she had just stepped out of the movies; every hair was always in place, her makeup always looked great, she wore nice clothes, and she always smelled so good. She was the sweetest lady that always had a lovely smile on her beautiful face, such an amazing woman that everyone just fell in love with her. I wanted to grow up to be as beautiful and sweet as my mom. I really looked up to her, not only because she was my mother, but she was so smart. As a kid, most grown-ups seemed smarter than me.

My father was tall, dark, and the most handsome man I had ever seen. His hair was always perfect, his clothes were always so nice, he smelled so good, he looked as if he could walk right of the movies himself. I felt like I was the luckiest girl in the world to have a father that was so amazingly handsome and smart. I thought he was smarter than mom, but I never would say that out loud.

My big brother was the cutest little fellow. He had blonde hair, blue eyes, chubby cheeks, and always had a smile on his face. One thing I know, he was very loved by both of our parents. My brother was always looking out for me; he was a great big brother. I feel in my heart that my parents were as proud and happy as they could possibly be.

Then, there was me, I thought I was a cute kid with blonde hair and hazel eyes; I have my mom's eyes. I always wanted to be as pretty as she was. I would get into her makeup and would have it everywhere except where it should be. I really felt, without a shadow of a doubt, that my parents were very proud of us and loved us with everything in them.

CHAPTER 3

Fun Family Things

We were always doing fun things growing up like going to Cincinnati Zoo. I have pictures of us with an elderly lady. I later found out that she was our granny. Everyone called her "Fat Granny" Fox. She would go many places with us because she helped our parents care for us. She was a very funny and very big lady. She was so big that when she would laugh, her whole body would wiggle like jelly. She seemed like she really enjoyed staying with us because she was always laughing in most of the pictures I have.

My mom loved taking pictures; she had lots of pictures of family and friends. We were always cooking out, having a bunch of people at our house, and kids playing outside with us. We also went camping; I saw pictures of other couples and many kids playing in the tents and the river. Most of the men would go fishing, and the women would sit on the blankets and watch us kids playing and swimming. The women would also sit around and talk about the men. I wish I knew who these people were so I could share some pictures with them.

We also went to visit my mom's sister, Charlotte, in Kentucky. She was married and had three girls. We didn't get to very much because we lived too far away.

CHAPTER 4

Pictures

Many pictures help me to recall memories of us growing up. There are a lot of pictures of this teenage boy that we don't know who he was either; he is outside playing with us in the yard.

I have the cutest picture of my brother. He had on a white vest with a red and blue stripe around the V-neck and was sitting in a little red convertible car. A teenage boy, who is in many other pictures, was standing with him. I also have a picture of me. It must have been Easter because I had the cutest purple dress on and a white hat, holding an Easter basket standing by the car where my brother was. I have pictures of Butchie riding me around in the car, looks like we were having a blast. Pictures are almost better than words because they don't lie, they are real.

In all my pictures, I looked like I was a happy-go-lucky kind of kid. I was always smiling and laughing. I was my daddy's little princess. I have a picture of my daddy holding me on his lap looking down at me with the proudest grin on his handsome face. I guess that is my favorite picture of us.

CHAPTER 5

Christmas

Our family had great Christmas celebrations together; it seems from the pictures I have. We never wanted for anything, everyone seemed to be enjoying themselves; they are smiling and have lots of love for each other. I have a picture of me with my little ironing board and iron, standing there looking as if I was really working hard. We all had lots of presents. As a kid, what else was there? I have lots of pictures of Christmas dinners with people I assume were my dad's family. In one picture, we are all sitting around the table with an older couple, I think they are my dad's parents. There were also two other guys in the picture I assume were dad's brothers.

Things seemed to be going well for us. Dad had a large family (three brothers—Johnny, Bobby, and Danny). He also had three sisters, June, Betty, and Marlene. I think they all lived in Cincinnati too. Mom's only sister, Charlotte, lived in Frenchburg, Kentucky, and was married to a man named Bill Stiltner. I just thought that was the funniest thing ever that sisters both had husbands with the same name, "Bill." Charlotte had three girls, Robin, Rhonda, and Karen. Mom and Aunt Charlotte had a half-brother named Mark who lived in Cincinnati too.

CHAPTER 6

Darker Days

We seemed like any ordinary family I had ever known. We would get up together, Mom would get breakfast ready, we ate together, Dad would go to work, and Mom would get us ready for school, then she would get ready for work.

When we came home from school, Mom would hurry to have dinner ready when Dad came home, and we would eat and talk about our day. Mom would clean up the kitchen and help us get homework finished and bathe us and get ready for the next day to start all over again. Daddy would always come in and give us a kiss goodnight and tell us he loved us very much. We would soon drop off to sleep.

When I was about six or seven years old, things started getting to be a bit different at home. We would still go to school and work, then we would come home like always. Mom would still cook and have it on the table for Dad. Then, he started coming home later and later, sometimes, we would eat without Dad which seemed to happen more and more. Sometimes, when he would come home, Mom would be sitting at the table crying, and then they would become so loud. Mom would get so angry at him, telling him that he would wake us up. It's like he didn't care because he would just get louder. Dad would eat, and Mom would sneak in and check on us, we pretended to be asleep because we didn't want her to think we heard them fighting.

Then, there were times when we would eat and be in bed when we heard Dad come in sounding like he was tearing the house down. Mom would start yelling, he would come in and tell us goodnight, kiss us, and say that he loved us. Wow, did he smell bad; not like he did when he would leave for work. He would leave our room, and Mom and him would fight and yell. It was a very bad feeling to try to go to sleep because we had to go to school the next day. It was getting to be an almost every-night thing, and it was getting so scary, not knowing if he was hurting Mom or if she would hurt him. She was a very small lady, but when she was mad, she could be very loud.

Then, late days turned into nights as Dad started staying out all night, then you talk about the fights and yelling when he did come home! I loved my dad, but he wasn't being a good husband or father because he had us all worrying about him. I would lay awake trying to wait for him to come home, but sometimes, I would fall asleep. I would wake up and run in the other room to see if he had come home because I remembered that he hadn't come in and tell us goodnight or anything. When I saw he wasn't home, I would worry, wondering if he had an accident or if he was okay. Then, we would have to get ready for school, but honestly, I couldn't do my school-work because I was still thinking of why my dad didn't come home. I would rush into the house looking for Dad after school without any luck. It would be days, even weeks, before he would come home. It was very hard on Mom trying to do everything by herself.

CHAPTER 7

Our Departure

After this had gone on for some time, Dad finally came home late one night, smelling as if he had been sleeping in a dumpster. Butchie and I were in bed when we heard a lot of screaming and glass breaking. Dad left and slammed the door, and Mom came into our rooms, threw our clothes in bags, put them in the car, and we left our house in the middle of the night. She said we had to be gone quick because Dad might come back and hurt or kill us. We were afraid to ask where we were going because Mom was crying so hard. We didn't know what was going to happen, not knowing where we were going or why Dad wasn't coming too.

That night, my life changed forever, and not for the better either. I knew something terrible had happened for us to leave in the middle of the night. Mom was very quiet driving, and I could see tears streaming down her face. She asked us to go to sleep because she didn't want to talk about anything, and she knew we were very tired, upset, and scared.

We kept looking out the back window for Dad, but we didn't see him. We had to stop at a gas station for gas, and that's when we saw Dad pulling in. Mom told us to run in the bathroom. Somehow, I fell, cutting my chin open. That's when the man at the gas station locked us in the bathroom until it was safe to come out. My Dad hurt the man really bad and was arrested. As we headed out of the bathroom back to the car, we were crying, watching the police take our father to jail.

Mom pulled out of the gas station and headed down the road. I was so upset that my Dad hurt the man, but he just wanted his family back. Mom kept telling him no that it wasn't going to happen, but he wouldn't leave her alone. I kept wondering what was going to happen to all of us. I was so confused, sad, and very emotional.

Butch and I finally fell asleep in the back seat, and when the car finally stopped, we were in Kentucky at my mom's sister's house. We all went in, and the kids went to bed. Mom and Aunt Charlotte were in the kitchen drinking coffee and talking, but not loud enough for me to hear, but I knew something was very wrong. Mom was crying so hard that I thought she was going to get sick. Charlotte kept telling her to calm down, that everything will be all right. Mom said she didn't know what she was going to do, how she was going to raise us by herself, but Charlotte said she was a strong woman and could do it, and that she would help her any way she could. They finally went to sleep for the night, but I could hear Mom crying.

At that moment, I wanted to wipe all her tears away. I was also angry at Dad because it was entirely his fault, but I felt so sorry for him because he was lying in a jail cell probably thinking how crazy he was to act like that to a stranger who was just trying to protect a woman and her children from a drunk loudmouth. I know it wasn't a nice thing to say about him, but the truth is the truth.

The following morning, Mom wanted us to sit down because she had something to tell us. She said that we were making a new start in life in Kentucky with our Aunt Charlotte and Uncle Bill until we could get our own place. I wanted to know why we couldn't go back home. I knew my Dad hadn't been very nice to her, but he could try to do better. I asked her that if I was bad, would she leave me too. I was so uncertain of grown-up stuff; it didn't make any sense to me at all. I asked her why he wasn't with us. She told us that he wasn't coming to live with us; that he was going to continue living in Ohio. I was so angry with her! I said that I didn't want to live there. I wanted to go home with my daddy. I told her it wasn't fair that I couldn't go home.

I was almost eight years old, and I didn't understand all this grown-up stuff, but as a small girl, I had feelings, and I knew exactly what I needed and wanted for my life. I wanted my family back and my old life. My mom said that we were never going back and that was all there was to say. I cried and cried because I was so angry at her. However, I knew that my dad was really to blame because of the way he would come home after drinking with the guys and him staying away from home for nights on end. I also blamed Mom for leaving the state and not asking Butchie and me what we wanted or even how we felt about everything.

My aunt and uncle welcomed us with open arms, although it was not the same as having your own family, I'm not sure how my brother felt, but I felt like a stranger. Even though they were family, we lived so far away that we didn't get to visit each other very much. There were eight people living in their small house. No one ever complained; we all just tried to make the best of a bad situation.

CHAPTER *8*

Our New Life

My brother and I had a very hard time adjusting to our new environment. We enrolled in a new school, which I hated very much. The little town was so small that everyone knew everyone's business. I felt like the other kids knew that I didn't have a father in my life. I didn't want anyone to feel sorry for me. I guess I was feeling sorry for myself. The teachers were nice and very helpful trying to help me catch up, but I wasn't really caring about school, only my daddy. I wondered where he was and if he was okay. I was a messed-up kid.

Don't get me wrong, Mom was great. I did forgive her, but I haven't forgotten. Mom got a job working in a factory in Mt. Sterling. She worked very hard trying to be both a mother and father to us. I felt very left out and cheated by God because he caused my mom to pack and leave Dad behind. I remember sitting looking out the window waiting for Dad to drive his old truck down the driveway so he could take me back home, but he never did. He never called. It's like he disappeared right off the face of the earth. I would ask Mom if Dad knew that we were in Kentucky. I would think that maybe he was in trouble, sick, or worse, dead. Mom would never tell us anything about him. I couldn't understand how things could change so drastically in one day, but it did for me. I found a picture of Dad, and I would hide and look at it and talk to him. I really missed him.

I blamed myself thinking I was such a bad girl that Dad didn't want to be a part of my life anymore. I would sit around trying to go over every inch of my life to see if I failed God or Dad or both. I couldn't remember anything that I could have done. I wondered what could a seven- or eight-year-old girl do that was so terrible that would cause your father to disappear out of your life forever. Also, what have I done to make God hate me so much that he would cause my life to be so wrong? I felt very guilty without even knowing why.

I started getting angry with everyone because I was feeling worthless and nothing but trouble. I had so many bad thoughts as a child thinking how a father could just walk out on his family and never look back; no phone calls, no visits, nothing at all. I wondered if he had an accident that had left him without a memory of us. I wondered if he knew how worried I was about him. I wondered if I would ever see him again and what would I say to him. Would I still be angry, or would I see his handsome face and cute smile and forgive him? I really didn't care about anything except the fact that I wanted him back in my life.

Feelings of abandonment are the worst feelings in the world, especially at such a young age. Being lost and forgotten by the man who helped me come into this cruel world; that was exactly how I felt, and no one could convince me any other way.

I was such an uncertain child always wondering if I would ever survive without my dad. I often wondered what type of person I would become being as helpless and hopeless as I felt. I felt like I would be better off dead, but I knew that my mother and brother needed me more than I needed to end my life.

Does anyone know how terrible it is as a child to lose your father, your home, family, friends, and everything you've ever known your whole life and move hundreds of miles away to live with a family that might as well be strangers? I was starting to panic, wondering if I should tell anyone about my feelings or just keep everything to myself. I felt like I should just be quiet and do as I was told because of the fear I encountered every day, wondering if we would just move again. If that happened, Dad would never be able to find us. I was always living with fear and deep depression.

CHAPTER *9*

Another Change

School was just like every other day, just getting by, pretending I was a happy kid. The truth of the matter was that I didn't know if I could go on one more day. It was so hard to act like you were happy about your life, like being at school, living in Kentucky, and then going back to my aunt and uncle's house pretending and faking my whole life to everyone. I knew deep down in my soul that I was the biggest liar in the world and the worst person. No wonder Dad doesn't want to live with us anymore. It's entirely my fault.

I prayed to God to take away all the anger that was built up inside of me. I wasn't only lying to everyone but myself too. Everyone was lying to me as well. God taught me that anger and lying were keeping me depressed, and I couldn't function. Too much stress and sadness for a child my age, so I had decided to try and change my way of thinking, I was really trying to be a better person.

Mom came home from work and said she has some good news to tell all of us. While eating dinner, Mom couldn't wait any longer to tell us. She had found a trailer that she could afford and was so excited about us starting a new chapter in our lives. I wasn't happy at all, I was so angry that I just wanted to scream at Mom by telling her that she had already ruined my life once by leaving Dad behind, and now, she wanted to move again so Dad wouldn't be able to find us. I ran out of the room angry and sad because she didn't understand why I couldn't move.

Mom came in to talk to me and asked what was wrong. I tried to explain to her how I felt, but when I saw the look on her face, she looked so happy and said that now we can have our own rooms again. We would be able to have friends over, but she didn't know I didn't have any friends because I didn't talk to anyone at school. I wanted to be alone. I tried so hard not to let her see all the tears that I had cried and how sad I really was. Mom was also sad; she never told us, but we could tell. She used to smile a lot like in all her pictures when we were with Dad in Ohio. She had been happy. Now, she was so tired from work and all the stuff she did for us that it made it hard on her to have a smile on her face.

I know she worked very hard to provide for us and to give us the best life she could. I tried so hard to be a good girl. Don't misunderstand me; I love my mom, and I also appreciate everything that she did to give us a normal life growing up. I wanted my mom to be happy too because everyone knows it's so hard for a single mom of two kids to work and be both a Mom and Dad. I really believe she missed Dad too; she just didn't want to admit it.

So the weekend came, and Mom and Aunt Charlotte cleaned up the trailer while we kids played outside. We moved in and gradually started buying things we needed to make our home as comfortable as possible. I knew that I would never be happy without Dad in my life. I haven't really felt safe since that terrible night we left Ohio. I kept thinking of that night when I was awakened in the middle of the night and dragged out of state away from my father.

Our trailer was very nice, but it wasn't like our home that we had with Dad. Our trailer was close to our aunt, so we still visited. We went to school, and Mom still went to work. Mom never stopped trying to make us happy in our new little place. As time passed, I noticed that something was still missing from her life. Mom was so beautiful, but her smile was missing, and she was very tired all the time trying to do everything for us and work at her job too.

Mom needed to be with other adults, not just us kids. She would come home from work and cook and clean, help us with homework, and make sure that we had our baths and were ready for the next day. Mom would pick up little things to make our place nicer. I know she would do things to keep herself busy, but we could hear her crying late at night when she thought we were sleeping. I know she missed Daddy as much as we did. I know how sad she was trying to raise two kids by herself. Mom had never complained about anything; she had been happy-go-lucky with us. After she was alone, she would work around the house and yard until exhausted to forget how sad she really was. Then, she would fall into bed and cry and fall asleep easily.

CHAPTER *10*

Our New Friend

Mom tried to do all the work around the house, but it was so hard because she was a small woman, so one day, after work and school, my aunt and uncle came by with this young good-looking man to help Mom around the house. Come to find out it was my uncle Bill's baby brother Olan that had just recently got out of the service.

Olan started coming around more, and we noticed the little looks and laughter between them. Mom had her beautiful smile back. I was happy for her, but then, I got really scared. Mom was happier than I had seen her since we left Ohio and Dad behind. The happier Mom became, the sadder I became. I know that sounds crazy because I wanted my mom happy, but I didn't want her to fall in love with anyone else because I didn't want her to forget about Dad wherever he was. I was trying very hard to keep my eyes open and my mouth closed. I kept thinking my dad was going to walk through the door, and that everything would be back to normal just like when we were in Ohio. My brother never said anything about Dad or Olan or even about living in Kentucky; he was always very quiet and very lonely. I tried to keep an open mind about things; I tried to pretend that we were going to be happy again.

Olan tried so hard to be good to us; he and Butch had a little special bond because Olan had a sharp blue Corvette. Olan did boy things with Butch, hoping he wouldn't miss Dad so much, but I know he did miss Dad. He wouldn't tell anyone how he really felt.

Olan started coming over for dinner more often, and we did a lot of things together like real families do, but it just wasn't the same for me. We did things with Uncle Bill and Aunt Charlotte and their girls on weekends. It should have been enough for me, but silently, it was killing me to have fun with the family while my father was out there in the world alone, hurt, or even dead, we didn't have a clue. But even then, I was determined to find him. I didn't care if it took me a lifetime to do so. I thought about my future a lot, wondering if I would ever be a good person, a good wife, or a good mother because I felt like I wasn't a good child because I lied to myself and everyone I came in contact with.

Mom finally had our place just as she wanted it. She had it decorated so cute and was very proud of herself. I was very proud of her too because she worked so hard. As a single, hardworking parent, she started from scratch to make a new home for us. My brother and I had our own rooms, decorated so nicely; we had everything we needed. We had a big yard to play in.

Christmas was approaching with no sign of our father, but Mom and Olan were doing well together. My brother and I had lots of presents under our cute little Christmas tree. We didn't have enough room for a very big tree because our trailer was small but big enough for us. I remember getting a new bike, an Easy-Bake Oven, other toys, and new clothes and shoes. I was feeling very blessed to receive all the gifts but sad for two reasons. First, Mom didn't have any presents, but she had a beautiful smile on her face as she saw how happy we were. The second reason was because of Dad, where was he? Was he alone? Was he happy or sad, sick or dead? Did he remember that he had a family? It was very hard to keep pretending that I was all right with my life. I would often wonder if Dad was thinking of us. Did he forget us? Was he looking for us? It was really hard to believe that someone who was supposed to love and care for you could just walk away and not even look back or call or just visit or send us a letter to let us know that he was doing good.

One day, in February 1969, Mom came home with a surprise. She was so excited. She had purchased a television set. She plugged it in, but it was so snowy that you couldn't see it. We weren't as happy about our surprise as we had been before Mom plugged it in. Later that evening, Olan stopped by, and Mom told him about the television. He laughed and told us that all we needed was an antenna and that he would bring us one on Saturday. So Butch and I started doing our homework, and Mom was cooking supper. Olan was trying to help us some, and then he would go in the kitchen and help Mom or pretend to so he could spend time with her. We would hear them laughing and enjoying themselves while cooking dinner.

Saturday finally came, and we were so excited. We helped Mom by cleaning our rooms. Mom wanted everything to be perfect, so she cleaned and was cooking a special lunch before Olan came to fix our antenna.

Butchie and I were outside riding our bikes and playing when Olan and Mom came out of the house to work on the antenna. Olan climbed on top of our trailer, and Mom was on the ground. While he was adjusting and placing the antenna to the right, he asked Mom to hold it up so he could brace it. All of a sudden, we heard this very loud, terrifying noise that ended up being a major accident.

CHAPTER 11

The Tragic Accident

After hearing the loud, terrifying noise, my brother and I ran around to the backyard to find our mother lying on the ground lifeless and not responding. We were scared to death! We were screaming for Olan, but he didn't answer us either. A man passing by in a truck heard the loud noise and stopped to help, but there was nothing he could do. He told us to stay away from the trailer, and he picked their limp bodies up and placed them in the back of his truck. in an attempt to get them help faster than waiting on an ambulance. Sadly, there was nothing anyone could do; they were already deceased.

Although my brother and I were old enough to know to stay away from the trailer, we were terrified. We sat all hugged-up crying as we waited on our aunt and uncle to come and get us. We were still young enough to know that something was terribly wrong. I didn't want to let my brother go.

Once again, my world was crushed. I had no father, now, I didn't have my mother, and even Olan was gone. I felt I didn't have any reason to live. Then, I thought I have a big brother that loves me so much. I have to be strong so I could protect him. My brother and I were suddenly orphans, and we didn't know what would happen to us.

I was young, but I did understand that when a person dies, that person will not ever be in your life again. I knew I would never ever see my mother again, but my dad was still out there in this big old ugly world. Just because we didn't know where he was didn't mean he wouldn't come and find us. I really believed in my heart that I would see my father again. I decided right then that I would spend the rest of my life looking for him. I just hoped that it won't be too late when I found him.

We really didn't understand exactly what had happened at the trailer. I guess the electric line was so low that when Olan raised the antenna up, it hit the electric line. Olan was electrocuted on top of the trailer. Mom was on the ground holding the pole, and the electricity running through the pole electrocuted her too.

I will never forget the smell of burning flesh; it was terrible. I wanted to scream out at God because, once again, he tried to destroy me. I was always taught that God loved his children, so if that was the case, why did he hate me? Wasn't it bad enough He allowed my father to disappear, and now, he killed my mother? Everyone always said that when someone dies, it's because God needed an angel. That was a lie because he was God, he had the whole world. Why did he need my mother? I will never understand how or why, but I guess that is the reason why we are not supposed to question God or his will for our life. I just know I hated him. I really would always think I'll just die and go to hell because I didn't have anything good to say about God. I wished he would just take me for an angel, but I've been so bad growing up that God couldn't stand me.

Chapter 12

Our Next Move

Once again, we were living with Aunt Charlotte and Uncle Bill and their three girls. Although I was so uncertain of how long they would be able to keep us because they were a young couple with three children of their own. Secondly, their house wasn't big enough for seven people. I have to give them so much credit because they were determined to keep us both together. I was so afraid that as orphans, we would be separated. I couldn't stand to lose my brother too.

As the days went on, I felt totally lost. I know that probably sounds crazy, but it's true for me. I was afraid of my own shadow. I guess I got it in my head that if I loved someone, they would die or just leave. I was even mean to my brother because I thought if I loved him, he would either die or leave me all alone. My brother was so sad, he felt lost too, but he wouldn't talk about anything. He was a loner and so was I.

The funeral was the worst ever. I didn't think I had ever experienced anything like that in my life. I saw my beautiful mother lying there in the casket with the most beautiful flowers I had ever seen. I would look at her and thought she was just sleeping. I wanted her to wake up. I know this is going to sound very weird, but as I looked at her, I thought I could see her chest moving up and down as if she was still breathing. I thought I was going to lose my mind. I felt like it wasn't really happening. I thought that if I could just take her out of the casket and take her home, she would wake up, and then we could be happy again.

So many people would come up and ask, "Oh, you poor little dear, are you doing okay?" I would just look at them and say to myself how stupid these people are! Did they actually think I would be okay with my mother lying there, knowing I would never see her again? I wanted to yell at all these people, but I remember Mom telling us, "If you can't say something nice, then don't say anything," so I would just look at them with a look on my face like "duh!" I hated people so much. At this point, I wished everyone would just disappear from the face of the earth. I know that I was taught not to hate people, but I hate their actions. I wanted to disappear myself. People would try to hug me, and I would just shrug them off. I only wanted my mom and dad to hug me.

The death of my mom and Olan was very hard on everyone. Such a tragedy! Two young lives were lost in one terrible accident! Olan was Uncle Bill's brother, so it was very hard on his side of the family. Aunt Charlotte and Mom had become very close after we moved to Kentucky, so this naturally was very hard on her too. We had a lot of people bringing food and sitting around and eating and laughing, and I was so upset because I didn't see anything funny about two people that I loved just a few hours earlier being put in a big hole in the ground and covered up with dirt. I kept thinking, *Wouldn't they be laughing and eating like a bunch of hungry wolves if it were their mom or brother?* People kept coming and hugging us like they have known us all our lives, but we didn't even know them. I thought, *Don't these people have anything to eat at their houses?* I just wished everyone would just go home and leave me alone. Finally, everyone went home, and it was quiet once again.

My aunt and uncle had a very small house, but they made room for my brother and me. I was so sad that I cried myself to sleep many nights. I tried to wait until everyone was sleeping, but my sweet aunt would hear me, and we would go to the other room, and she would let me cry, and she would hold me until I couldn't cry any more tears. My aunt said she understood how I felt because she and my mother had grown up without their parents. She told me their mother didn't want them, so she posted an ad in the newspaper giving them to anyone who wanted them. I thought, *What kind of mother could give their own children away?* A couple from Kentucky took them and raised them. I thought my mom and aunt must have been very sad thinking they weren't wanted by their parents. I also thought that maybe my mom didn't want us either, but everyone said that God wanted her instead. I couldn't believe that because God could have anyone and everyone he wanted, so why my mom?

Although I didn't want to go back to school, I knew I had to. The first day back, all the kids were whispering about me. My teacher told the kids to stop talking about me. She was a very nice teacher, so since she had told the other children to be quiet, they started calling me the teacher's pet. I was a very shy and quiet child. I stayed to myself, so I didn't have to talk to anyone or answer any questions from anyone. I felt like it wasn't anyone's business because they didn't talk to me much before the accident, so I thought they need to leave me alone and mind their own business.

I missed my father and mother so much that I couldn't understand why God was punishing me again. First, he had made my dad disappear out of our lives, and then he thought he needed my mom in heaven instead of being with us. I knew God hated me. I wasn't too happy with him at this point. I would sit in class and wonder about all these things and cry all night until I was a mess. I have never ever felt so alone, low, and so depressed in my life. I was always thinking of different ways of getting my life back to normal, but honestly, I really didn't know what normal was anymore. I felt like I was crazy and no good to anyone or myself.

CHAPTER *13*

A Day to Remember

One day, while I was sitting in class trying to do what the teacher had wanted us to do (honestly, I couldn't help it; my mind wasn't into studying), I heard a lot of commotion in the hallway, not sure what it was, but it was loud, someone beating on the door. My teacher went to the door, then she stepped out into the hallway to try to find out what was going on. I knew that someone was very angry. As I sat there listening to them argue, I knew that it was important. The teacher came back into the room and came over to my desk to tell me that I was wanted in the principal's office. As I walked down the hallway, my knees were shaking so hard that I didn't think I was going to make it. I knocked on the door, and as the door opened, I saw my brother and my aunt and uncle. I was very confused at why everyone was there. I thought, *What now?* I was scared that they weren't going to keep us anymore. I knew I hadn't done anything wrong. I tried so hard to be a good kid.

Then, I thought for a minute, and I knew it wasn't my uncle being loud in the hallway, so who was it? Then, I found out that it was my father! He had heard about my mother being dead, so he came to get us, but no one would let him see us. I really felt cheated once again because I think that my brother and I should have been able to see him, which was all I ever wanted. Because my father had a very bad background with the police, they decided that it would be better for us to stay with Charlotte and Bill. They were only trying to protect us from being hurt again, but no one knew how much my heart was breaking all over again.

One thing that made me feel good was that he did want us. He was trying to be a father to us again, but no one would let him even try. I also remember being so angry because I felt like everyone was trying to ruin my life for me, and I didn't like it at all. It was so unfair! I couldn't help but think about Dad during all of this. Was he trying to fight for us and his rights as our father? Was Dad scared of losing us for good or never seeing us again? I know I was terrified that I wouldn't ever see my dad again. I was so sad and hurt as my life kept getting worse by the day. I would wonder what would happen next.

Life went on, but it wasn't really mine. I went through the motions each day without the emotions I needed to feel. Have you gone through something that you didn't feel right? Well, every day was like for me. I was so numb and empty inside. I was really what older people called a "basket case." Everything seemed so unreal to me like a bad dream or a nightmare that I couldn't wake up from. I really felt in my heart that I needed a hospital to help me sort out all the bad things I was thinking and feeling, but I knew that everyone who was talking about me since I moved to Kentucky would just start talking about me being crazy. I knew I wasn't crazy, just confused about my whole existence in this cruel world which I was tossed into.

I had so much hatred in my heart about my life, my missing family, and God. God hated me, and honestly, I didn't like him at this moment either. I looked back at family pictures, and I was always smiling, and I seemed like I was very happy, but when you lose everything, it makes a person a very unhappy person and fills you up with hatred and anger without even trying. It also causes you to have a heavy heart, and it makes it hard to smile or live a normal life.

Have you ever watched a movie when someone has the best life in the world? That's how I had felt before all my losses. I had wonderful parents, a big brother, a nice house, and everything I ever wanted or needed until it all came quickly to an end. I had lost Dad, my home, friends, family, then Mom, our new home, and all my dreams and my life. I really wished I could have died too!

CHAPTER 14

My Search

My fourth-grade teacher was so wonderful to me. She understood my pain, my loss, my confusion; it's like she knew how I felt about my life. She asked me what my father's name was and where we lived in Ohio. She also wanted to know my mother's name and where I was born. She would search for him looking in the newspaper and every place she could think of. She looked in the phone books and made so many long distance calls for me. I tried to explain to her that I didn't have any money to pay her back. She told me that it didn't matter and that my happiness was more important than a few dollars.

I had to have an operation on my ear and stay in the hospital for some time. I wasn't sure how long I would be out of school, but my teacher didn't want me to get behind in my classes. She came to the hospital and brought me homework, stayed there while I did the work, and helped me when I needed help. She was such a great teacher and a person whom I felt so comfortable telling her all the things that were on my mind. Teachers have a huge responsibility with all the students, but it takes extreme dedication to go way beyond the classroom. I really loved my teacher! Her name was Mrs. Henry.

Chapter 15

My Punishment

Have you ever heard of people being punished by God? Well, I really believed in my heart that I was being punished. I started to believe that I was switched in the hospital. Maybe I was not really the daughter of my parents, and I might be the daughter of the devil.

The first reason was because we lived together as a family: Dad, Mom, my brother, and I. Then, we had to move and leave Dad behind, never seeing or hearing from him again. I thought that when two people wanted to spend the rest of their lives together and have children, you just couldn't walk away from them and the responsibility of seeing them grow up and enjoy being a family. Not this time. God saw other things for us, not for the good for me and my brother.

The second reason, God took my mother and her friend away to be an angel. God was punishing me for something. I couldn't figure out what I did to make him so angry, If I did something wrong, why didn't he just take me? Then, I thought I couldn't be an angel because I was the devil's daughter and couldn't go to heaven.

I remember a preacher saying that people can't do wrong and get by with it because God knows and sees all. Well, I started taking it to heart. I was really starting to think that I was the reason Dad wasn't living with us anymore. I also felt so guilty because it was my fault that God took Mom and Olan to heaven. I was so afraid that my brother would be the next one taken from me.

At that moment, I vowed never to love anyone ever again because it was way too painful. I felt like I wouldn't be able to live if I lost anyone else at this point in my life. I continued to go to church, but it was very hard to understand when I still blamed God for my ruptured life. I tried my best to be good and listen to what my elders told me, but I couldn't believe that anything I heard was true.

I went to school, but I didn't do very well because it was hard for me to stay focused on schoolwork when my heart and life were extremely messed up. I tried to keep to myself so people wouldn't ask me any questions or feel sorry for me. Everyone knows how cruel kids can be, I knew firsthand, that's one reason I didn't like people very much.

Don't misunderstand things, my aunt and uncle were very good to us. They opened up their home and hearts for us. They understood our situation. They tried so hard to make a happy home for us. Nevertheless, I didn't want to get too close to them or anyone. I did everything I was told to do because I was young but afraid that if I was not a good kid, I would be sent away from my brother, and my dad would never find me. It was a scary feeling to think that if you messed up, you could be moved out to another home and with strangers once again.

CHAPTER *16*

Forgiveness

Finally, I came to the point where I had to forgive God for everything that went wrong in my life. It was hard for me to go on day after day with the hatred, misery, and the disappointment I had. I went to church and learned that God was in control of my life, but I had to let him. I had to trust that he knew what was best for me. I had felt so unworthy of anyone's love, especially God's love, because of the guilt that I grew up with. I know that I had great parents and a new wonderful family. I just had to learn to trust and love and appreciate what they were doing for me and my brother.

The bible says we are not to be envious and jealous of what other people have, so I had to realize it meant that I shouldn't let it get to me because I didn't have my own parents. God saw fit to give me someone else that loved us just the same. I had several Sunday School teachers telling me that God wasn't angry with me and that none of this was my fault. Also, the problems adults have aren't caused by God but by them letting the devil take control of their lives. All couples have problems, but they don't let their children know because they don't want to worry the children with grown-up stuff. They also told me that Mom's death was a freak accident.

We did a lot of church activities like going to camp which was so much fun. We learned a lot about God and stuff, but we also had softball games, lots of different sports, and campfires. We learned a lot of songs. I let God and church be my life.

CHAPTER *17*

School Starting

School was starting again, and I was really excited to try to make a fresh start. I was feeling better about myself, and I thought it was a new year where kids might have forgotten all about my life. I was a different person even though I have not forgotten any of the bad things that have happened or my parents, but Dad was still out there somewhere, and I still had not given up on finding him. I learned at an early age to never give up on things you want because, with God, all things are possible, so I knew one day it will happen.

I always knew in my heart that I would always have a loving home with Bill and Charlotte, but I wanted to make things easier on them. Whatever they needed help with, I tried to do it. We all would clean our rooms, get ready for school, have breakfast, and clean up the kitchen before school. After school, we did homework. We lived on a farm, so we had chores to do outside. I loved being outside doing things because it gave me thinking time.

I loved sports, so I played basketball, ran cross country, and track. I was tall and skinny. I thought I was pretty good at everything I tried to do because I thought it would just be a waste of time if I didn't do my best at everything. I loved running because it was something I could do by myself and think of all kinds of things. I called it my alone time. I went from being scared to being very confident. I let God be in control, and he helped me with all my problems.

CHAPTER *18*

Growing Up

Well, as the years went on, I continued in sports and church and grew as a nice young lady. I didn't do that well with my grades but mastered the sports. I really enjoyed them, it was my escape from reality; don't get me wrong, I ended up being a level-headed lady. I felt like there was nothing in life that I couldn't handle. I learned a lot about life and death. I knew I wanted to help others, not financially but emotionally and physically. I wanted to become a nurse after I graduated from high school. Not sure if I could do it because of my grades, but I vowed to really work hard if I were accepted into a good college.

Well, I finally made it to the twelfth grade, and we went to different colleges and did reviews to see what we were interested in. I wanted to go to Midway College because they seemed to have the best nursing program, and they also had a basketball team. I was really excited about college. I just wondered if I could do it, but I really wanted to try. As time went on, the more scared I was getting.

We had prom, and my aunt made my dress, and it was so beautiful that I felt a lot like Cinderella. I had long blonde hair, and I thought I was pretty. I was talking to a guy that didn't go to school anymore. He quit, I guess that should have been a clue, but guess what? It wasn't. Getting back to the prom, I was asked to go with another guy from my class, but I said no, but we danced and had a good time. I felt a little guilty, but not enough to have a good time.

Then, there was graduation. I made it. I was so proud of myself, but I kept thinking that I wish my dad could have seen me walk down and receive my diploma. I never ever forgot about him, wondering if he ever thought about me and my brother. I always had it in the back of my mind that I would find him. I also received a full scholarship to any college of my choice for my basketball playing. I was so excited but nervous, afraid that I wouldn't be good enough to play with the players and teams.

CHAPTER *19*

Big Decision

Well, it was time to make the decision, going to college or getting married. I made the wrong one. I gave up the scholarship and my dreams because I felt like I wasn't a very good student. I really had to work hard to pass in high school, and I couldn't think about failing and being kicked out of college and making my high school and my family down, so I chose not to attend school at this time. I thought I could always go to school at a later time.

So my wedding day was approaching so fast. My aunt made my dress, and I never saw a more beautiful dress in my life. She was so wonderful to me. I wish my mother was there too, but I know she was watching me from Heaven. I really missed my father walking me down the aisle. My uncle gave me away, that was so nice of him, but it just wasn't the same. I couldn't help being sad, I know that was supposed to be a happy day, but under the circumstances, it was hard. I wondered what Dad would think of the choices I had made. Would he be disappointed? Although it was a beautiful wedding, and I was happy about most things, I was just wondering if I would regret it as time went on. I just needed someone to love me and for me to love.

CHAPTER 20

My New Life

Things were going really well for us, we had jobs and a nice place to live, thanks to Bill and Charlotte for allowing us to pull a mobile home on their land. My husband's parents helped us buy a mobile home. We seemed to be getting along really well, but I was kind of sad because I wanted more. I still was missing something in my life. I wasn't sure why I was feeling this way. I think I was wondering if every marriage was this way. Jeff was very understanding because he knew all about my past, and he knew I have had a long search for my dad, and he was willing to help me all he could; that really made me feel good about things.

We spent a lot of time on the phone checking with people who had the last name "Dobbs," but it was like everyone we called would tell us the same thing. We went on a site that was called US Search; it gave us a list of every name and number and addresses of anyone named William Eugene Dobbs, William Dobbs, and Bill Dobbs in all the states, but we called and called so many people that we ran the phone bill up really high, and it was hard to pay it. We found a few names that had addresses but no phone number, so we would take a few road trips and go to the people's houses. We didn't have any luck, but I really did appreciate his willingness to help me. Sometimes, he would have to work so I would take off and go to Ohio all by myself, and sometimes, a friend would go with me, but we still never had any luck. So we would slack off searching for a bit and work and make extra money so we could look again. We did this for years without getting any closer. I was beginning to think it was too late. At this point, I was getting very discouraged and depressed, but I wasn't going to give up by any means. So as the years went on, we continued our search without any success. I really needed something else in my life. I wanted a baby, so we began trying, although I was wondering if I would be a good mother or if my husband would be a good father or would he run off leaving me to raise my child on my own, but I was willing to give it a try.

We ended up having a son, and he was the perfect, cutest little thing I ever saw. He was a handful; very mischievous, always into everything. As he grew, he was so cute; he had blonde hair, blue eyes, and gets tanned very easily. He was so loved, but I was extremely sad because my mother will never ever see what a beautiful grandson that she would have had, and she would have been so proud to call him her grandson. Then, as always, I would think about my father and wished I could find him so he could see his grandson. I know he wasn't the nicest person in the world, but I always believed in forgiveness, and I would think about people changing when they lose everything in their lives that gives them a reason to want to become a better person.

Andrew was five, and then we had him a little sister, Sarah. He really loved her and was so protective, but he would always get a little on the jealous side when people who made over the new baby he would act up, get into stuff. She looked just like him with blonde hair and blue eyes. It was so long since we left Dad. I couldn't really remember what he looked like, and I couldn't really remember Mom either, but I knew that my babies were so beautiful. I just wished my parents were still around and be able to see them.

We would take rides to Ohio looking for my father. We would stop at all the gas stations along the way and look at the phone books for my maiden name and if there were any that we could call and see if they were related to my family. Sad to say, we didn't have any luck.

We continued on our trip, then we would go home, and I would feel so lost again. I would get depressed. I wouldn't talk about my feelings. I just would keep them inside and try not to let my feelings

WHERE'S MY BIRTH FATHER?

get in the way of being a good mother. I had already decided that I wasn't a very good wife. We fought and argued a lot, and things just continued to get worse. I really am not proud of the fact that my husband and I would really get into several fights. Then, of course, I wondered if everyone did, but I never saw my aunt and uncle fight, so I knew it was just us. We would go to church and fight all the way home; it was very hard to try to live for God and then argue all the time.

CHAPTER 21

Another Departure

After twenty-one long years of marriage and arguments, I decided that I was not only being unhappy, but I felt like my children weren't happy either, so I chose to leave. My son was seventeen, and my daughter was twelve, and it was really time to part ways. I asked my son if he wanted to go with us. He said no, he wanted to stay with his father. My daughter and I went to a town called Shelbyville, Kentucky. I got a job at McDonald's, we did fair but still weren't as happy as I should have been.

All my friends seemed happy with their husbands and lives; I kept trying to figure out why I couldn't be happy. I always kept thinking of the life I had lived and realized that it was because I didn't really belong anywhere. I had shared a nice family of other children; everything in my life was always about someone else. First, I was my mother and father's child, and then I was an orphan, then I was the niece of my aunt and uncle. I really appreciated everything they had sacrificed for my brother and me. As we all know, when we marry someone, we become their spouse, and I almost forgot my name because I was Jeff's wife. Then, the children came, and as they grew up, I became Andrew and Sarah's mother.

I was still trying to find out who I was and what I needed to do in my life to be a happy person once again. I've made so many mistakes on this long journey. I felt like I hurt my children staying in a relationship or marriage that was such a mistake from the start, but

I know that we all learn from our mistakes. I know I have, but you can't change the past; only make our future better.

My son was very upset by us leaving, and for a few years, he would tell everyone that I had died because to him I had, even though I asked him to live with his sister and me; he refused. I think he felt like I had left him and not his father, but trying to convince him was something else. Children can be very hurtful when it comes to not wanting to admit the truth about their parents.

I look back at the time when my mother had left my father. I understand she was trying to protect us, living with the fighting, and arguing the children have a lot of guilt, wondering if they were fighting because of us or something else. I know that it wasn't easy for me, so I'm sure it was hard on my mother either.

I don't want to make it sound like it was all my husband's fault because only the Lord above knows why I was never satisfied with my life. I had two beautiful children and a good job making decent money. I didn't really want anything; even what my children wanted or needed, they had. Andrew lived with his father, but we finally got past the reality that I wasn't happy and needed to start a new life.

CHAPTER 22

The Struggle

Many years have passed, and more mistakes have been made, including getting remarried. Then, the true colors finally came out about him, so needless to say, I didn't stay married to that mistake very long. I was still missing my father. I never wanted the feeling of defeat but with two failed marriages and the struggle of moving away and starting all over once again. At this time in my life, my daughter had graduated from high school and was working. She had her own apartment, so I decided to move to Somerset, Kentucky.

I found a job at a local day care center cooking and taking care of the kitchen. It wasn't the greatest job, but the pay was decent, and the people were really nice. It wasn't long before my daughter decided to move to Somerset too. I was excited that she was moving close to me again. She started working at the day care center also. She loved taking care of the children. All the children loved Sarah; she was really good at her job. She stayed with me until she met what she thought was the man she wanted to spend the rest of her life with.

Andrew was still living in his Dad's house, working and doing very well. He met a young lady he wanted to marry, she had three children Andrew was really good with her children. She was the best thing for him because he did have a wild streak, and she settled him down.

Both of my children were very happy. Needless to say, I was the one who still hadn't found the thing that was going to make my life complete. I was always driving to new places trying to find anyone who knew my father or any of his family without any success. I was getting so depressed.

I would go to work and go home and didn't do much except get phone books from all the places I could. I met this man, and we had an ongoing relationship for a while, and things, I thought, were going so well. I was really falling for him until the day came when he told me that his mother was sick, and he had to move to another state to take care of her. That made me sad but, again, made me happy that he cared so much for his mother that he was willing to give up his happiness and take care of her. I wished my mother was around to have someone to take care of.

Then, I realized what I wanted to do with my life once again. I worked in nursing homes, hospitals, and houses that had three or four patients where I was a house manager. I loved the job and decided to go back to school to become a nurse. While I was in school, I had a car accident that kept me from finishing my classes. I had a long recovery, but I still had my job when I was able to go back to work. Work was going really well for me. I had three patients in the home and had a couple of awesome girls working with me. We had the best house that the company had, and we took the ladies out to eat, to parks, and to the movies.

Chapter 23

The Secret

It's kind of funny the way things worked out. I worked long hours, and if someone couldn't work or show up, I would fill in because they had families at home. I wanted my girls to be happy, so I would give them lots of time off due to the fact that I had no one at home. It worked out really well.

One day, one of the single girls told me about this website called "Tag" for meeting people. One day, I went home and checked it out. You had to download this app, and I'm not good with computers. I had a very old laptop, and it was so slow that I didn't use it very often. One day, after work, my friend came over, and we set up a profile on the site. I started chatting with one guy. He was so cute, and I loved his profile, so I would race home and try to chat, but my computer was so slow. Sometimes, it wouldn't even let me get on the site. I just decided to give it up until I could buy another computer.

About a week later, my daughter came to the house, and I was still working, so she called, and I told her I would be home soon and just continue waiting for me. She opened up the laptop and saw that I was chatting with this guy. His name was Louis, so she started chatting with him pretending to be me. He asked her where I had been, and she said I was working many hours. She told him so much stuff about me, but she forgot to tell me that she was chatting with him. He lived in Tennessee, so when I got home, she told me she was just checking her e-mails. I didn't think too much about it until a few days later. I came home one day and got on the computer and saw the message from him asking me why I didn't chat much. I was a little worried that if I told him I had an old computer, he would think I was strange or poor, so I told him anyway because we were taught to be honest even if it was not the thing we wanted to say. Of course, he started writing "haha." I'm like, "Why did you do that," and he said, "I do computer repair, and I sell computers too." I had agreed on my next day off to meet him in Oneida, Tennessee. I had planned to buy a computer. So finally, Sarah decided to tell me that she was chatting with him pretending to be me. She said she was trying to keep it a secret but was afraid that when I met him, I would find out because he would know stuff about me that I hadn't told him, so the cat got out of the bag.

CHAPTER 24

Meeting Maybe Mr. Right

Well, I drove to meet Louie in Tennessee. Needless to say, I had never driven to Tennessee before, so I got lost and ran out of phone service, freaking me out. I started thinking I had made a huge mistake. I didn't tell anyone in case it was a big flop and that he wasn't as cute as his profile picture. I didn't want anyone to think I was crazy, but I was starting to think I was. It took me four hours, and I worried he would think I had stood him up. I was also concerned that he wouldn't be there, but he was standing by the pay phone with the cutest grin on his face. I asked if he had thought I had stood him up, and he laughed and said no. He knew I would show up sometime. We went to Shoney's for a meal and talked for a while. We exchanged numbers, and he put the computer in my car. He wouldn't let me pay for it, and I didn't want him to give it to me. He was so cute and sweet.

Although we had jobs and we lived in different states, we continued to talk. He came to visit me, and we would go to a restaurant and talk. We agreed that he could do his computer business in Kentucky, and we wanted more out of our relationship, so he moved to Kentucky to be with me. I had a nice small apartment, and we really enjoyed each other's company. We had a good life together.

A week or so, after Louie moved in, his grandchildren called him from Tennessee and needed him to come and get them because they were staying with one of their mother's friends. He was really stressing out about what he was going to do because he had given up his house, so together, we agreed to go get them. We made out in my little place for a short time. The children were very sweet and adjusted well. When Louie's daughter came to live with us, it was time for a bigger place. We moved to a house, and we all loved it. Our children and grandchildren really got along well, and we were a big happy family.

Louie opened a booth at the flea market selling computers and repair services, and he did really well. I liked to sell things too, so I opened up a booth across from him. It was really fun, and we met a lot of nice people. Louie would try to help me look for my dad, and one day, we were talking to a friend. She was telling me about a website that I had heard of before called Ancestry. She said that I have to pay to get on the site, but she was already a member and gave me her password and let me use her account. I couldn't wait to get home so I could search for my dad. I stayed glued to the computer every spare minute.

Louie's daughter and the children moved to Illinois to where their mother lived, and the house seemed too large for the two of us. We also wanted to buy something of our own instead of renting. Louie liked it in Kentucky, but I think he missed it in Tennessee. We would go to Tennessee, pick up computers and items for resale, and we went to auctions. Gatlinburg is a very wonderful place, and the Smoky Mountains are breathtaking. Louie and I thought it over and decided to move there because it was a nice place. We kept our flea market booths in Somerset, Kentucky, since we were making good money, and my daughter and grandbabies still lived there, and it was only an hour and a half away.

CHAPTER 25

My Anticipation

One day, I was looking on Ancestry, and when I put my father's last name in, I saw different people that were related. I started looking at pictures of some of these people and saw a picture of this young man who looked like he might be graduating from high school. I couldn't get the image out of my mind. I knew I had seen this picture before but couldn't quite put my finger on where, so I went to my box of pictures that belonged to my mother. I kept looking until I found the same picture, but I didn't know who it was. I was determined to find out who he was but wasn't sure how or what I was going to do, but I was so excited; that seemed like it was the closest I have been in so long. I was so completely happy.

I got back on the computer looking for any clues that I could find about this guy and found that his name was Ron Halcomb. I saw the same picture and asked him who it was. It was his cousin's graduation picture, but unfortunately, he was killed in a car crash. He said his name was Danny Dobbs, and I said my mother has the same picture in the box of pictures, and that my last name used to be Dobbs. So Ron called another cousin, and she called me, and that was the happiest day of my life! I know when you get married, have children, and have other life celebrations that those are very happy occasions, but this was better for me.

My distant cousin Cindy told me all about my father's family. He had three brothers and three sisters. I had a family I could call my

48

own. I still didn't know where my dad was at this time, but I knew he was still out there, and I was more determined than ever to find him. Cindy's mother was named Marlene and had passed away, so I knew I wouldn't ever meet her, but I was so thankful for my cousins Ron and Cindy. Cindy had three sisters, Teresa, Brenda, and Lisa. Cindy also told me about Aunt Betty who lived in Florida. She had a son named Jimmy and a stepson named Paul. I couldn't wait to meet them all. Aunt June, who lives in Ohio. She also had two sons, Tony and Joey, who have passed away. Someday, I planned on taking a trip to see all of my new family. Uncle Bob has passed away, so I won't get to meet him or his family. Dad's other brother, John, all I knew about him was that he lived in North Carolina, but I hoped to meet him as well. Danny was the baby, and I already knew that he had passed away too young, never had a chance to have a family.

CHAPTER 26

The Call

One day, I received another call from Cindy telling me that Aunt Betty wanted Cindy to give me her number, so I called Aunt Betty. We talked about a lot of things and for several hours, and she was being as honest as she could be. She had no idea where my father lived, but when he called her, she would tell him that I found and contacted her and that I had been searching for him for my whole life and that I was so wanting to get in contact with him. She told me that he always called her on holidays, and Christmas was coming up, so she thought that he would be calling soon. She wanted me and my husband to come and see her. I was so ready to pack my bags and go to Florida, but I had a job taking care of an elderly lady, but I knew where I was going to visit when I had some time off from work.

My aunt and uncle in Kentucky decided to have Christmas on January first, so Louie and I were just having an average day at home. He was in the basement when Aunt Betty called to wish us a Merry Christmas and to give me my dad's phone number. I literally screamed at the top of my voice when I hung up the phone with my Aunt Betty. Louie flew up the stairs as fast as he could. I think he took two steps at a time. He said, "What is wrong? Why are you screaming? You scared me to death!" I said sorry and told him that my Aunt Betty called Dad's number, but I was so scared that he wouldn't want to talk or that things would go wrong. I was crying so hard. I was excited and scared all at time.

I pulled myself together, and I gained my composure and dialed his number. When he heard my voice, the first thing he said was, "Is this my baby girl?" I was so happy that things went really well, and we talked for hours. We laughed and cried and talked about meeting. He said it was snowing hard where he lived which was in Florence, Kentucky. I was on cloud nine after forty-five years of searching. I called my brother, but he wasn't really as excited as I was, but no one was going to spoil my Christmas gift. I also called my daughter and told her, and she was so happy for me. This was the best day of my life! I couldn't wait to see him and find out what had happened and where he had been all these years. I was a little worried about what my aunt and uncle would think and me finding him and getting to know him.

CHAPTER *27*

My Journey

January second finally rolled around, although it seemed like it would never come. It's like the old saying "A watched pot never boils." Louie and I got up early and started out on our journey to meet my father. It's a three and a half drive, but at this moment, I would have gone to the moon and back to see my father. I was so nervous and excited and scared but happy as I can be. Dad called early and asked if we were still coming, and I said, "Of course, we are." He said they had a little bit of snow but not much. I was so glad that Louie is used to driving in the snow because I'm not a very good driver even when I wasn't nervous.

We went straight to Dad's house, we walked in, and the first thing Dad said was, "Betty?" I said, "No, Dad, it's me," and he said I looked just like his sister. Then, he gave me the biggest hug and kissed my cheek. He was so thin and feeble, I wasn't sure if it was because of his age or if he was sick. I was hoping he wasn't sick. Then, the next thing he said was to take my shoes and socks off. I started laughing because I've never had anyone want to see my feet, but I did, and he said, "Yeah, this is my baby girl 'cause her feet are just like mine."

We exchanged gifts and ordered pizza. We had such a good visit that I didn't want to leave. He showed me pictures that he had always had in his wallet. One was my mother in a white nightgown, and it was so elegant that I thought it looked like her wedding dress.

The other pictures were of me and my brother. Dad bought me a beautiful necklace with a heart and a key. I thought it was the most wonderful gift in the world.

I told him all about Butch and his children, and he was hoping that Butch would have come with us, but he was still not happy about me meeting him. He was afraid that Dad would only want to take things away from me. Dad wasn't even like that. He may have been that way in the past, but after losing everything, he had ever loved and had people changed. I showed him pictures of Butch and his family and pictures of my children and my grandchildren. He thought they were so wonderful that he couldn't wait to meet them all. He had tears in his eyes but quickly looked away. I told him that the past was gone, and we can't change any of it. We just have to move ahead.

Dad had a woman living with him but only as a roommate. Her name was Janet, and she seemed very good with Dad. She cleaned and cooked and made sure Dad took his medicine on time. They had a beautiful house. He had a new pickup truck and seemed to be doing very well for himself. I was really happy that he seemed to be doing good, and he seemed so happy too.

We had a small black lab named Lassie, and my dad had a very large black dog. They played together, but we thought it was cute that we had the same kind of dogs. Lassie loved my dad; he would sit by him while Dad spoiled him. The dogs both loved playing with toys. We laughed so much about everything that my jaws hurt. Finally, they went to lay down and slept, so we went back to talking about everything.

I could tell that Dad was getting tired, and he didn't want to say anything because he didn't want us to leave, but we had a long drive ahead of us, and we had to work the next day, but it was worth it all. We planned on making another trip soon. We continued to talk every day on the phone. It was as if we both knew we needed to do this bonding.

I constantly continued talking to my brother telling him that Dad was getting old and how he really missed us and was so sorry that he wasn't there for us while we grew up, how he had tears in his eyes when he was showing me the pictures of us that he had carried in his wallet for forty-five years, and how he loved our mother. He asked me for Dad's number, but I wasn't sure if he would use it, but I was hoping he would.

Two weeks later, Butch did call Dad and agreed to go visit him. Dad called me, and he was so happy that he was going to see Butch after all this time. My family was making its way back to being normal except that Mom wasn't there to see the change in Dad and the happiness that meeting him has changed me. I knew where I belonged after all the years of feeling that I didn't belong anywhere in this world.

Butch went to see Dad, and they had a really good visit, did a lot of talking about guns and knives; all the men stuff. Butch told Dad all about his children and looked at all kinds of pictures. They went to take a drive to where we lived in Ohio. Dad showed him a lot of places; he couldn't drive like he used to, so he had Butch drive his truck. Janet couldn't drive, so Dad didn't travel much unless one of his friends took him out. They had a great time. I was so glad that Butch decided to forgive Dad before it was too late.

We all kept in touch; I planned a birthday get-together for my dad's birthday. Sarah and her family came, Dad got to meet Sarah's kids (he loved watching the kids play), Louie made a big pan of spaghetti, and we had cake and ice cream. Everyone had such a good time. Dad didn't want any of us to go home, but the kids were getting tired, and everyone had to work the next day.

Andrew didn't get to come this time, but we planned on getting together a lot more often because we all had a lot of catching up to do.

Louie and I went back to see Dad several times. I was so happy; I finally felt like I had a place in life, I had a family of my own. Louie was so patient with all the trips back and forth; Dad really liked him a lot. I had the hole in my heart that was finally getting filled with love. I really respected my father for wanting the best for us, even though I didn't agree that it was the best, but Dad says, "Father knows best."

Chapter 28

Thanksgiving

I had so much to be thankful for because I had my own family. I was so excited every time my phone would ring. I talked to my dad and my aunt Betty and my cousin Cindy quite often. I felt like I finally knew my place in this world. We went to my dad's for thanksgiving and had a really good visit, except for one thing, I realized that Dad didn't eat very much, and he was getting skinnier and gets tired more easily. I asked him if he was sick. He really didn't want to tell me, but he had cancer. He said since we hadn't had much time to get to know each other, he didn't want me to worry about him, which, of course, I did.

We spent the night, and Louie woke up early and cooked breakfast. Dad didn't eat and said he didn't feel very good. We took him to the hospital, and they said his cancer had spread through his entire body, and they ordered hospice. My heart was broken. I knew that it was just a matter of time before he was gone, and I would be without him again. The hospital sent him home, and I knew that I had a job at home, but I wanted to stay and take care of him.

We had Dad all settled and helped Janet get everything needed to make him a good place for him to rest. I wasn't sure how Janet would be able to take care of my Dad, so Louie and I talked about it all the way home. I was going to put my job on hold, go, and stay with him and take care of him. I knew that for every day we had left, we could share stories about all the years that we hadn't been in each other's lives.

That night, when we got home, I called my boss and explained the situation to her. She said that she understood and didn't blame me at all and asked if I could help her find someone who could take my place until I could return. I felt much better about being able to go stay and help my father in his last days. My boss's brothers wanted to send her mom to a nursing home, but she said no and that she would do whatever she had to do to keep her mother at home with her; that's how I felt about my dad going to a nursing home.

We went to bed, and I had everything on my mind. I was so tired, but I kept trying to think of someone to work for me. I finally dozed off to sleep when my phone began ringing, and I was wondering who could be calling in the middle of the night. It was Janet saying that Dad had fallen and broke his hip, and he was in the hospital. The doctor had operated on his hip, and I knew that the cancer would spread after they cut him open. I called my boss telling her about Dad falling and breaking his hip and that I would be going to be with him in the morning. I felt bad because I hadn't found anyone to help her with her mother, but she told me to go ahead and go help him because he was going to need me more than she needed me to help her. She said my family needed me, and it made me feel important.

Needless to say, I didn't sleep much that night, but I was up early the next morning, packing my clothes, and calling my kids and my brother about Dad falling and that I was going to be staying with him for a while. I wasn't sure how long we would be able to exchange stories of things we encountered while being apart for all these years. I was a little nervous too, not really knowing what to expect. Louie stayed a few days before he had to go back home.

CHAPTER 29

Hospital Stay

Dad had to stay in the hospital for a week, but he was in very good spirits. My cousin Ron came to see him while he was in the hospital. He and Dad had a very good visit. I enjoyed meeting him because I didn't know any of my dad's side of the family. The doctor told Dad that with his health, the way it was, physical therapy wouldn't help much, but I didn't agree. I think as long as you want to get better and are able to walk, you could. The hospital was a really nice place, but Dad said he was ready to go home.

Janet didn't go to the hospital to see Dad. She said she needed to be home getting things ready, but honestly, when we went back to Dad's house, I couldn't see anything that she had done. I wanted to be there when the doctor came in to talk. Dad had a lot of other medical problems, so I wanted to talk to them and find out everything I could so I could give him the best care possible. I loved my dad, and I wanted him to be able to go home and rest and spend what time he had left so his friends and family could come and see him.

I rearranged Dad's bedroom so that he could use his wheelchair, bedside commode, and bedside table; everything that the hospice helped us with to make him comfortable. The hospice nurse came and went over all Dads' medications and stuff with me so I would know when he needed to take them. The nurses were all really good at their job and were a very big help to me as well.

I knew that Janet wouldn't be much help for me. I don't want to talk poorly about her, but I found out that she was slow, and Dad had another woman living with him for many years. She was Janet's aunt, and Dad made her a dying promise to help Janet as long as he could; to take care of her and give her a place to live, so Dad was trying so hard to provide her with everything that he had promised.

Janet was a very sweet lady, I really admired her for everything that she was doing to try and help Dad, and I was so glad that she had called me when he fell and was hurt. She felt comfortable allowing me to come in and take over with his care. We really became friends and were making the house ready for Dad to come home.

CHAPTER *30*

Dad's Homecoming

Today was the day that Dad's coming home from the hospital. I drove his truck to go pick him up, and yes, he was really ready to come home. I was a little bit scared about driving his truck because it was bigger than my car. I also wasn't sure how capable he was of being able to get in and out of the truck, but I was willing to get him there. The first thing he wanted to do was get a sandwich and a piece of pie from Frisch's Big Boy Restaurant; that was his favorite place to eat. I thought that was really weird because that's me and my daughter's favorite place too.

We arrived at Dad's house, and our trip was good; he never made me nervous at all. I got Dad in the house, and the first thing he wanted was his dog. He told me the story of him falling and how his dog saved his life. He went outside on the porch watching it snow because, where he lives, they get lots of snow. As he was turning to go back up on the porch, he fell on the steps and couldn't get up. Janet was in her room and maybe sleeping or had the TV on, but she couldn't hear him yelling her name. He passed out from the pain and lay on the steps for so long that he was covered with snow. He looked at his watch, and it had been two hours since he had fallen. The dog continued to bark, and after several more hours, Janet finally heard the dog barking. She opened the door and saw Dad lying in the snow but couldn't help him up, so she called 911, and they took him to the hospital. Dad said that's why his dog was his hero and his best friend.

My dad was an amazing man not to have gotten upset with Janet. I'm sure I wouldn't have been that nice. I was kind of angry with her because she was supposed to be watching out for him, not letting him fall outside and stay in the snow with a broken hip for hours. If Dad wasn't angry with her, I should just keep my mouth shut,

The awesome thing was that Dad was home and enjoying himself telling the story of the accident. He was sitting in his recliner and watching TV when the hospice nurse came and made sure that he had everything he needed to be comfortable. He told her yes that his baby girl was taking care of him. I didn't want him to get too tired, so I was keeping him resting. He asked me where I was going to sleep, and I told him I had fixed up the extra room and cleaned it up.

The next morning, he wanted me to call Louie and Butch so they could come and see him, so I did that. We planned a visit for the weekend, and he wanted me to go to the store and get stuff to eat. I went shopping, and he did get some of his appetite back. I told him that I was not a good cook and that Louie was our cook at home, and he was really good at it. Louie didn't wait for the weekend; he came up and cooked lots of different dishes that we could put it in the freezer. That way, we would have good food all the time when he was at home. He was so sweet; my dad thought he was wonderful. Louie and Dad hit it off just like best friends.

Dad told us so many stories about Mom and Butch and our life together many years ago. He told us that he would take me and Butch to the store, and Butch would want candy, and I only wanted a dill pickle. He would laugh and say that the pickles were bigger than I was. I told him that I still loved dill pickles, and both my kids love them as well.

CHAPTER 31

Christmas with Dad

I had the best Christmas ever. Dad was getting weaker every day, but he couldn't wait for us to have Christmas together; me, Butch, and him, the only person missing was Mom. We talked about Mom. He said he loved her so much, but it wasn't her fault; they were young, and he was stupid. I told him he wasn't stupid, but he said he lost everything that meant anything to him. Dad told me that he knew all about us while we were growing up. He moved thirty minutes away. He told me all about the ball games I played and the temper I had. He said I got that from him. He also told us about watching me run in track and cross country meets. He also watched me walk in at my proms. I would have loved to know that he was there, but he said he thought we would be better off not knowing. He wasn't the best person; he did so many things that landed him in prison several different times. I learned so much about him and his life, I told him so much about mine as well.

Dad never did marry anyone else; he wasn't as stupid as I was. I told him about my two failed marriages. I kept telling him that I didn't want to do it again, afraid of failing again. I was always very competitive and didn't like to fail. I also told him how I felt growing up feeling guilty, worthless, and very much unloved by God. He told me that I shouldn't feel that way because it wasn't anyone's fault but his. I didn't want him to feel bad, so we changed the subject. I'm not sure what all Butch and Dad talked about, but I know they were both at peace with the past. They had made plans to do things as Dad felt well enough.

Dad, Louie, and I talked about buying a motor home and driving to Florida to see Dad's sister Betty, the one that Dad said I looked like. I told Dad that we had gone to see Aunt Betty and how amazing she was. We had a great time visiting with her. Dad said he hoped that she hadn't told any bad stories about him. We laughed and told him we couldn't tell him until we were all sitting face to face. Dad talked to Aunt Betty a lot on the phone; they seemed so close. Dad told Betty all about our plans to visit her, and she was so excited. She said it had been so long since she had seen him.

Well, unfortunately, we had to call it a night, my brother had to go home. Dad didn't want him to leave, but he had a young daughter and wanted to spend time with her on Christmas. Dad was very tired, so he called it a night. Louie, Janet, and I cleaned everything up before going to bed. I felt Dad had a good time with us all. I know my dad had children with other women because he had told me, but none of them called him to wish him a Merry Christmas. I thought that was strange, but I really didn't want to share my time with Dad on Christmas.

CHAPTER 32

New Year

We started out with a new year with Dad. He was getting weaker and sicker. I was so glad I met him and the time we have together. It's getting harder every day seeing him decline more and more, but the good thing was that Butch brought his children to meet Dad, and he enjoyed meeting his grandkids and great-grandkids. Dad met Sarah and her boys, but little Sarah wasn't born yet. Andrew never had a chance to meet Dad or bring his son to meet him; that was a little depressing to me, but at least one of my parents met my daughter and grandkids.

Louie asked my dad if he had a problem if he asked me to marry him. My dad told him he needed to make an honest woman out of me. They talked a lot of things when I was in the other room. Dad really liked Louie, he told my dad about my other marriages, and he said it's a good thing he wasn't able to get out because they would pay for putting me through all the drama that I went through. Needless to say, he wasn't happy with them at all. He made Louie a promise that he would treat me like a queen. Louie said he couldn't treat me any better than he is. Louie is a very good man and does spoil to death. All I had to do was say I liked something, and it would be at the house the next day. Not too many men would allow their girlfriend to go to another state and stay with someone they really didn't know, and he would travel back and forth from Kentucky to

Tennessee on a regular basis, bring me clothes, and come and cook food for the week to make it easy for me.

Louie had to go back home, I missed him when he went home, but I understood he had work and stuff to do and that he worries about our house when no one was there. We would talk on the phone every chance we had. One time, Dad was sitting in the living room watching TV, and I was on the phone, and I was holding it on my shoulder, and my dad said, "Give me that phone, you are going to make your neck stiff," so I gave up my phone. I was fifty-five years old and grounded from my phone. I thought that was so funny that he was always making me laugh. I knew that he wouldn't be around too much longer. He was getting so weak and was unable to walk much. He was using his walker, but he's starting to use his wheelchair now, but he sure hated someone pushing him, dressing him, and doing everything for him. I would tell him that I would do anything for him. I told him that I searched all my life for him, and I was so blessed to have met and gotten to know the real man that my mother loved enough to start her family with—even though things didn't work out for them. He still loved my mother more than his own life.

Dad told me all about their life together and how sorry he was and that he wanted so many times to come and get us, but he said he would see us always smiling and seemed to have everything we ever needed. I told him how I felt so cheated by God and that I should have the right to choose who I wanted to live with, but he said that he was such a bad man and had been in so much trouble with the police in many different states that no judge would ever let him have anything to do with us, so he chose to change his social security number and moved to Mt. Sterling so he could keep an eye on us. I told him there was nothing he could ever do to lose the love I had for him.

Dad told me all about the plans for our wedding; he wanted to give me away and because he didn't get to the other two that I had married. He said he couldn't walk me down the aisle. I told him that I would push him down the aisle because I wanted him to be there and to give me away. He asked Louie to find a house so he could go to Tennessee to live with us. I was so excited that I could take him home and take care of him there, and he would be there for our wedding.

CHAPTER 33

Valentine's Day

Dad was trying to be sneaky; he knew Louie was on his way, and they had been making plans without me and Janet knowing. We had a good morning. I was checking out wedding dresses, and Dad wanted to see all of them as I was looking. We found a few that we both liked, so when Louie came, he wanted him to take me to try them on and buy one. We went, and I didn't like the way any of them fit, so we went back to Dad's, and it was snowing, so Louie was going to go to the store for groceries. He wanted to cook us a special dinner. Dad's favorite was meat loaf, and Louie's meat loaf was the best.

Louie came back from the store, and Dad wanted Louie to come into his room, so Janet and I were watching a movie. So then, Louie came out of the room and started cooking, and we helped peel the potatoes, and Janet said Dad loved beets, so they were chatting and cooking, and the home health nurse came, and we were in Dad's room. She told him that he needed to stay in bed because he was getting too weak, and he told her we were moving to Tennessee. She said he couldn't travel, and he was heartbroken. Dad told Louie what the nurse had said, and he told Dad we could get him to our house if that's what he wanted to do. He said, "Let me think about it for a bit." He was really tired, so he wanted to take a nap, so we were all in the other room.

Dinner was completed, and we went to ask him if he wanted to come into the living room to eat, and he said no and that he would just eat in his room; it's like he was different after the nurse left. We fixed him a plate, and he wanted to watch boxing, so we let him stay in his room and eat and watch TV.

After dinner, he told Louie to get our stuff. He bought Janet flowers and a box of candy and a necklace. They bought me flowers, candy, and a cute heart necklace. Louie had to go back home, so he left soon after we had eaten, so Dad kept asking me if Louie had made it home yet. I told him I would let him know when he was home. It was snowing really hard, so I was nervous about Louie being on the road, so I went outside and was shoveling the driveway and the sidewalks, just trying not to let Dad see that I was upset. I thought that if Dad saw me, he would think it was his fault that I was unhappy, but it wasn't. So I heard from Louie he had made it home, and I went in to tell Dad. He said he was glad, and he wanted to look out and see the snow, so I helped him to the window, and he saw it. He said he wanted to get ready for bed, so I took his dishes to the kitchen. I was really happy because I thought Dad had eaten all his food, all except for the beets. Dad was all ready for bed, and I went to get his meds for the night. He said he would take them. He wanted to see Janet, so she was in his room, and I told her to make sure that he had taken his meds; she said she would. I was doing dishes and just finished, and Dad wanted to see me for a few minutes. I enjoyed all my minutes with him, even though they were getting shorter and shorter.

Dad told me how proud he was of me and how he knew Louie would take good care of me, and he appreciated him for letting us spend all this time together. He was just so kind that he hugged and kissed me and asked if I had a Happy Valentine's Day today. I told him yes. I did ask him if he had, and he said, "Every day with you is wonderful." He told me how much he loved me and how he was so glad the day Betty told him about talking to me on the phone and that I wanted to talk to him; he said that it made his Christmas too. He asked to call Louie, and he thanked him for coming for the day and cooking and getting the candy and flowers and necklaces for us. He told him he loved him. I was so happy about everything. I didn't see the red flag.

Dad went to sleep for the night. Janet and I were watching TV when we heard a loud noise, and I jumped up and tried to run down the hall, but she didn't want me to, so I just shoved her out of my way. I walked into Dad's room and turned on the light. To my shock, there was blood everywhere. I yelled for Janet to call 911, but she wouldn't. She was going to call her brother, and he lived in Ohio. I was holding a towel on his head, and I called the hospice and called 911, and the police and ambulance came, and Janet acted so weird; I didn't know what to say. I called Louie, and he drove back. I followed the ambulance with a friend beside Dad's house, and Janet wouldn't go to the hospital.

Dad was a "no code" but didn't want to be kept alive on the machine, so I told them to take him off. I knew he was gone, but he hung on for the longest time. I was trying to figure it out, but I finally thought he was waiting until after midnight because he didn't want to ruin my Valentine's Day. At two minutes after midnight, I told Dad I loved him, and he could go be with Mom, and he slowly quit breathing. I said my goodbye and left the hospital in Ohio and sadly went back to the house.

I wasn't sure who I wanted to blame, the hospice nurse or Janet because I know she gave him the gun and never said a word to me about what he wanted to do. I was really upset, and then I went into Dad's room and shut the door. I just needed to be alone. My mind went back to the day I watched my mother take her last breath. I knew Dad was in a large amount of pain, and the nurse told him it was just a matter of time, and he didn't want me to see him go downhill every day.

I finally came to my senses and came out of the room to find Janet and her brothers and other people going through my dad's stuff. I asked them what they were looking for, but they never really said anything. I told Janet that Dad had asked Louie and me to watch out for her, but she said she was going to go live with her brother, which was good with me because I still had hard feelings toward her. She said she didn't give him the gun, but I knew she was the only one who could have. Police said I couldn't do anything to her, so I let her get what she wanted out of the house, and my brother and Louie came. We cleared out the house and went home without Dad.

Chapter 34

Dad's Final Wishes

My dad never wanted a funeral or anything about him posted in the newspapers. He had already made all the arrangements years before he passed. After he was cremated, we took his ashes back to Tennessee with us. He wanted his ashes to be put in Lake Cumberland in Somerset, Kentucky, but I wasn't ready to let him go yet.

I had so many mixed feelings about what he had done. First, I felt it was wrong of him to do that to me because I was willing to take care of him until the end. Secondly, I felt he did it to protect me from the embarrassing moments of me having to bathe him and clean him after he had an accident. The chaplain at the hospital told me that when a cancer patient is in so much pain, they forget about how it might hurt others, but they just want to end their pain. Also, I asked the chaplain if someone did what Dad did if they are going to hell. His reaction was that they are in so much pain that they don't comprehend their actions, and sometimes, when the person doesn't die immediately, they have time to ask for God to forgive them. I know when I told Dad that it was okay to let go and to be with Mom. He just slowly quit breathing. I was so sad, but I know he isn't suffering anymore.

It was extremely hard to adjust to not having Dad around. I kept thinking I could hear his bell ringing because when he needed or wanted something, he would ring his bell. I had Louie to help me through all of the grieving process. We talked about Dad a lot, and

I felt it really helped me. He told me some of the stories that Dad had told him about me. I would laugh then cry for a while. He told me that Dad wanted to be at our wedding, but I almost didn't want to get married because Dad couldn't be there, but I knew he would want me to move on. I kept remembering all the times we spent together.

Louie and I finally picked a wedding day. We decided on Father's Day in remembrance of Dad. We were married at an outdoor gristmill with the waterwheel and an old building. It was beautiful, and I knew Dad would have loved it. I had a table set up with Dad's urn and a picture of Mom and him on each side and a poem I had written many years ago so that they were both at our wedding.

If anyone is searching for a lost family member, lost loved one, or someone who you care about, don't give up because you won't ever feel complete. You will always say, "Why I didn't do this or that." You won't be able to spend time with the person before it's too late. Never give up on your dreams because life is too short to give up. I never had a real place in my life until the day I saw my dad after all the years of looking, hoping, and dreaming. I still have my dad's ashes. I'm just waiting for the right moment to say goodbye.

ABOUT THE AUTHOR

Deborah Dobbs Riggs has written this book to let the readers believe in themselves as a person, as a daughter, as a son, and as a parent to know that anything is possible as long as you have the faith and dreams. Deborah has become a caregiver in order to be able to help families in need of assistance with their parents. She believes it's because she missed her parents so much as a child. She really enjoys spending time with the elderly and listening to the stories about their families causing her happiness because she felt she would meet her father and spend hours listening to him telling stories of her life with him as a child. Deborah has had patients she stayed with for eight months day and night, not even going home. She has so much compassion and love to share. She hopes reading this book helps in many ways. It has taken many years to write this book, but with the grace of God, it is finished.

CPSIA information can be obtained
at www.ICGtesting.com
Printed in the USA
BVHW030315160322
631525BV00004B/524

9 781637 104569